Dental Hygienists

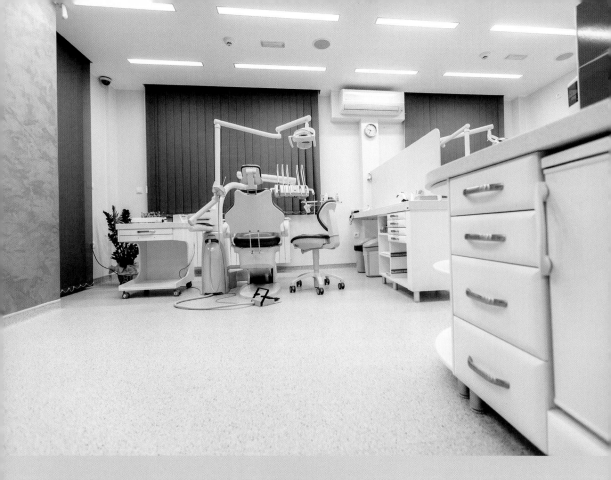

Careers in Healthcare

Athletic Trainers
Clinical & Medical Laboratory Scientists
Dental Hygienists
Dietician Nutritionists
EMTs & Paramedics
Nurses
Occupational Therapists
Orthotists & Prosthetists
Physical Therapists
Physician Assistants
Respiratory Therapists
Speech Pathologists & Audiologists
Ultrasound Technicians

CAREERS IN HEALTHCARE

Dental Hygienists

Jennifer Hunsaker

MASON CREST
PHILADELPHIA

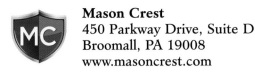

Mason Crest
450 Parkway Drive, Suite D
Broomall, PA 19008
www.masoncrest.com

©2018 by Mason Crest, an imprint of National Highlights, Inc.

Printed and bound in the United States of America.

CPSIA Compliance Information: Batch #CHC2017.
For further information, contact Mason Crest at 1-866-MCP-Book.

First printing
1 3 5 7 9 8 6 4 2

Library of Congress Cataloging-in-Publication Data

on file at the Library of Congress
ISBN: 978-1-4222-3797-7 (hc)
ISBN: 978-1-4222-7985-4 (ebook)

Careers in Healthcare series ISBN: 978-1-4222-3794-6

QR CODES AND LINKS TO THIRD-PARTY CONTENT

Table of Contents

KEY ICONS TO LOOK FOR:

 Words to understand: These words with their easy-to-understand definitions will increase the reader's understanding of the text while building vocabulary skills.

 Sidebars: This boxed material within the main text allows readers to build knowledge, gain insights, explore possibilities, and broaden their perspectives by weaving together additional information to provide realistic and holistic perspectives.

 Educational Videos: Readers can view videos by scanning our QR codes, providing them with additional educational content to supplement the text. Examples include news coverage, moments in history, speeches, iconic sports moments and much more!

 Text-dependent questions: These questions send the reader back to the text for more careful attention to the evidence presented there.

 Research projects: Readers are pointed toward areas of further inquiry connected to each chapter. Suggestions are provided for projects that encourage deeper research and analysis.

 Series glossary of key terms: This back-of-the book glossary contains terminology used throughout this series. Words found here increase the reader's ability to read and comprehend higher-level books and articles in this field.

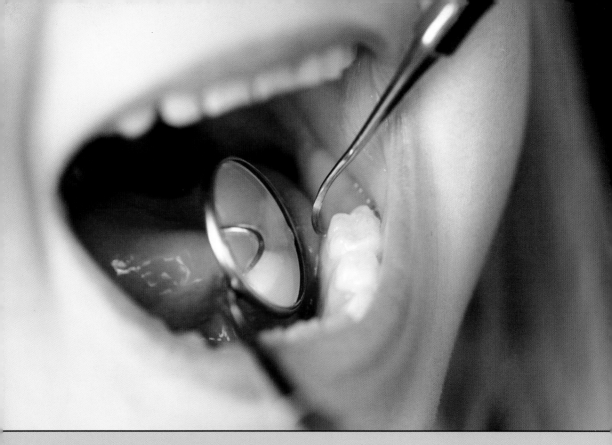

A dental hygienist checks a patient's mouth for signs of periodontal, or gum, disease.

 Words to Understand in This Chapter

anesthetic—a drug administered to patients to make them numb to pain.

calculus—a hard, calcified deposit that forms on the teeth and contributes to their decay.

fluoride—a compound applied to the teeth to prevent tooth decay.

intangible—not having a physical presence that can be touched or seen.

plaque—a soft, sticky deposit on teeth in which bacteria grow rapidly.

sealant—a thin, protective coating that prevents tooth decay in the grooves of a person's teeth.

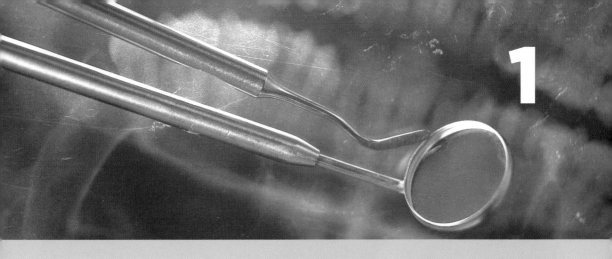

1

What Does a Dental Hygienist Do?

For many people, going to the dentist is hardly the highlight of their day. The tools are loud, you cannot see what is happening, and you know you haven't flossed well over the last six months. However, the majority of the interaction that takes place is not between the patient and the dentist, but between the patient and the dental hygienist. Valuable members of the dental team, dental hygienists are the first people to see a patient and they play a vital role in setting them at ease, performing diagnostic testing, cleaning their teeth, assisting in their dental procedures, teaching them how to care for their teeth, gums, and mouth, and performing general office tasks.

Avoiding sugary drinks is one thing dental hygienists encourage their patients to do.

Diagnostic Testing

Before a general dentist or an orthodontist examines a patient, a dental hygienist performs a variety of tests. These tests not only determine the health of a patient's teeth, gums, and mouth, they also give the dentist the information he needs to do his job.

A dental hygienist, sometimes referred to as a dental assistant, reviews the patient's medical history for changes that would affect her oral health. This may be in the form of discussing changes in health status or making notes in the chart for the dentist to review.

A dental hygienist also takes x-rays on a patient's mouth. This allows the dentist to see any evidence of decay in the patient's teeth below the gums. The type of equipment used and the number and variety of x-rays varies between offices, but in each case the dental hygienist is responsible for ensuring that x-rays are taken, developed, and placed in the patient's chart. In many offices, a dental hygienist may need to take impressions of the teeth and mouth to help other professionals create retainers, bridges, crowns, or caps.

Finally, dental hygienists perform visual screenings for oral cancer in the mouth and gums. They will then use tools to assess the patient's gum health between his teeth and his tooth health below the gums.

Cleaning Patients' Teeth

The ultimate goal of any dental hygienist is to help her patients have the best oral health possible. Periodic professional cleanings help patients maintain the health of their teeth and gums

My First Dental Hygienist Job

A dental hygienist working in the field told this story about her first experience working as a dental hygienist.

"My father was a dentist, so I grew up around a dental office. From the time I was 12 or 13, I would earn money cleaning the office at night. I worked the front desk when I was 16. I learned how to clean and sterilize the dental tools and I did that until I graduated from high school. My whole life, I knew exactly what I wanted to do. I went to college, got great grades, learned everything I could learn. I did well in clinicals. I was fairly confident that I could do the job well.

"But I remember my first day at my first job very clearly. I sat with my first patient and suddenly thought, 'What in the world am I doing here?'

"I quickly realized that, while my education prepared me well for being a dental hygienist, while my experience prepared me for working in a dentist's office, there was still so much more to learn. I was lucky to work for a dentist who had been a dental hygienist before she went back to school. She was the ideal mentor for me. She pushed me to be better, taught me how to refine my clinical skills, and shaped me into the hygienist I would become. But I will never forget that feeling of being on my own for the first time. It was frightening and exciting all at the same time."

by removing soft deposits and hard deposits. A dental hygienist is trained to remove *calculus* (also known as tartar), *plaque*, and stains from a patient's teeth. Using a variety of tools, dental hygienists remove these deposits above and below the gum line. They then use an ultrasonic tool to polish the teeth. Dental hygienists also routinely give patients treatments to prevent cavities, such as *fluoride* and *sealants*.

In some states, dental hygienists can perform oral care procedures, such as cleaning and removing plaque and tartar, without the collaboration or supervision of a dentist. In these situations, dental hygienists may own their own practice, where several dental hygienists clean patients' teeth but refer patients to dentists for fillings and more complex procedures.

Since patients spend more time at home caring for their teeth than dental hygienists do in their office, patient education is one of the most important things a dental hygienist does.

Dental hygienists must spend time charting their patient's x-ray results, signs of disease, and procedures.

In most states, dental hygienists can clean a patient's teeth in hospitals, clinics, nursing homes, or even schools without a dentist's oversight.

Assisting in Dental Procedures

Dental hygienists are trained to assist dentists with a variety of procedures. They can help dentists make and insert crowns, do fillings, and extract teeth. They can be trained to help periodontists create bridges, do veneers, and place tooth implants.

In many states, dental hygienists can administer sedation, such as nitrous oxide and local *anesthetic*, to make patients more comfortable during procedures. Dental hygienists can also be trained to assist orthodontists in placing and adjusting braces, creating expanding appliances, or otherwise managing the positioning of a patient's teeth.

Educating Patients

Dental assistants spend more time with patients than anyone else in the dental office. This

Educational Video

For a sneak peak at the daily life of a dental hygienist, scan here:

means they can educate their patients in a way that dentists cannot. They may teach children and adults proper brushing and flossing techniques, likely counseling their patients to brush and floss more frequently. They may give patients plans for how to quit smoking and otherwise preserve their oral health. In some cases they may even teach their patients how nutrition plays a role in the health of their teeth and gums. Ultimately, dental hygienist are not only health care professionals, they are teachers as well.

Doing Clerical and Office Work

When a dentist sees hundreds or even thousands of patients each year, there is no way to keep everyone's needs straight. Every action performed in a dentist's or an orthodontist's office must be written down. Whether this is done on paper or

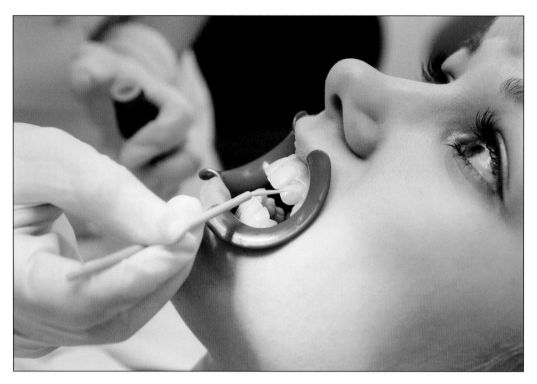

Fluoride products help to prevent tooth decay in children and adults.

in a computer, dental hygienists take the lead in maintaining their patients' charts. Not only is this documentation important for insurance billing purposes, it also enables dentists and hygienists to keep track of the progress a patient is making, the types of procedures performed, and any medical conditions that may impact a patient's oral health.

A dental hygienist may also be given tasks like cleaning and sterilizing instruments, preparing workspaces, maintaining the office, and placing follow-up calls to patients after procedures. Each of these tasks ensures that the dental office runs smoothly and patients have the best experience possible.

A Softer Touch

Few people are excited to visit the dentist on a regular basis. Widely considered the nurses of the dental world, dental hygienists play an important part in easing patients' worries. They explain the procedures they perform, the tools they use, and the pain-relieving options that are available to patients. Their collaborative relationship with dentists allows them to explain, in easy-to-understand terms, the types of care patients need. They also provide a listening ear for patients' concerns and offer helpful suggestions to help their patients make the most of their oral health. Empathy and compassion are some of the *intangible* qualities necessary for a successful dental hygienist.

 Text-Dependent Questions

1. Why are dental assistants widely considered the nurses of the dental world?
2. What are the diagnostic tests a dental assistant may perform?
3. In what ways do dental hygienists educate their patients?

 Research Project

The next time you visit the dentist for a cleaning, ask the hygienist to explain how he or she uses the various tools to clean teeth.

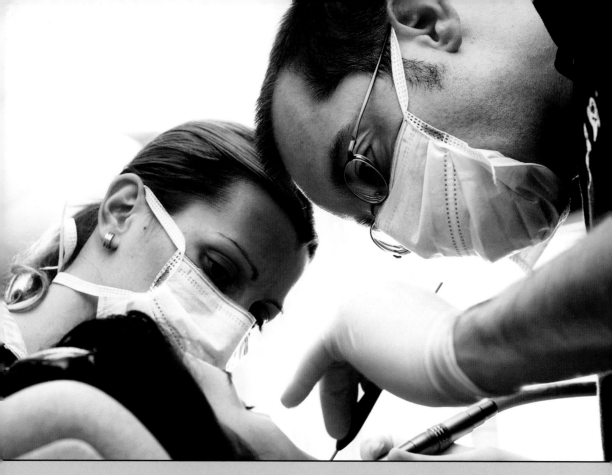

Most dental hygienists work in dentists' offices.

 Words to Understand in This Chapter

clinician—someone who has direct contact with patients, rather than conducting laboratory studies.

endodontics—a branch of dentistry concerned with the study and treatment of the dental pulp; endodontists also perform root canal procedures to save teeth.

periodontics—a branch of dentistry concerned with the structures that support the teeth, and with treating gum disease.

prosthodontics—a branch of dentistry concerned with the design, manufacture, and fitting of artificial replacements for teeth.

ultrasonic—referring to a tool that vibrates at a frequency above the speed of sound.

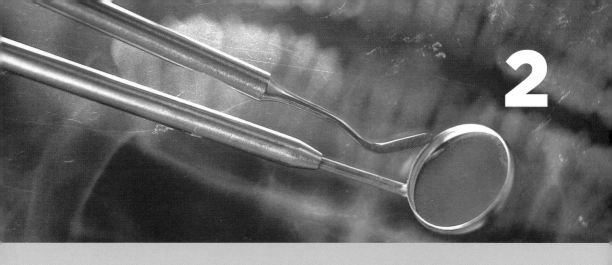

2

A Look at the Opportunities

More than 200,000 dental hygienists were working in dentists' offices in the United States in 2014. According to the U.S. Department of Labor's Bureau of Labor Statistics, that number is expected to increase by 19 percent over the course of the next decade, much faster than the average for all other professions. It is believed that ongoing research linking oral health to overall health will continue to spur the demand for dental hygienists across the country as more people seek dental care.

Dental hygienists can take one of several career paths. These include work as a *clinician*, in corporate sales, in public health, as a researcher, or as an educator.

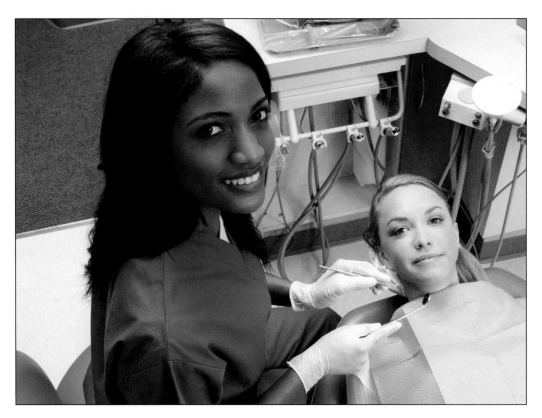

Half of all dental hygienists in the US work part time, and in most cases they work for more than one dentist.

Clinicians

Dental hygienists who work as clinicians are usually employed in a general-practice dentist's office or an orthodontist's office.

Almost all dental hygienists work in a dentist's office. Here they examine patients for signs of oral disease, perform dental cleanings, and teach patients how to care for their mouth, teeth, and gums. About half of all dental hygienists worked part time in 2014. Since most dentists hire hygienists to work a few days a week, hygienists may work for more than one dentist.

Dental hygienists use many different tools to do their job. They clean and polish teeth with power, hand, and *ultrasonic* tools. They may use lasers for tooth whitening. They may also polish teeth with a tool that works like an automatic toothbrush or remove stains with an air-polishing device. Dental hygienists use x-ray machines to check for tooth or jaw problems that cannot be seen on visual examination.

Dental hygienists also work in specialty dental offices, such as those of pediatric dentists, *periodontists*, *endodontists*, and *prosthodontists*. Pediatric dentists work with children who often require special anesthesia; this calls for additional training. Endodontists are dentists with additional post-graduate training to work primarily with the inner, soft tissue of the teeth. Prosthodontists replace teeth with temporary or permanent replacements. In all these cases, dental hygienists assisting these specialists may receive further on-the-job training to perform dental hygiene tasks in their offices.

Orthodontic Dental Hygienists

When patients arrive in orthodontic offices, the orthodontic dental hygienist helps make the patients feel comfortable and shows them how to clean their teeth and braces. Orthodontic dental hygienists also help orthodontists identify problems and changes in a patient's mouth. They may perform x-rays of a patient's jaw and teeth. They may also create molds of a patient's bite so braces, retainers, expanders, or other orthodontic appliances can be made.

Orthodontic dental hygienists prepare tools for an orthodontist to use. They ensure that these tools are sterilized and in place before and after a procedure. They also keep a patient's mouth clean and dry during procedures and assist the orthodontist during procedures by handing the orthodontist the appropriate tools.

Orthodontic dental hygienists teach patients how to care for their braces, retainers, and other appliances. They may instruct patients on how to care for their teeth and gums while they are wearing braces, as well as what to do if their braces or retainers break or become uncomfortable.

Corporate Dental Hygienists

Corporate dental hygienists work for companies that support the dental industry. In many cases, this involves the sale of products and services that are designed to help general-practice dentists, orthodontists and other specialists, and dental hygienists do their jobs more efficiently. Dental hygienists' clinical experience and understanding of the way dental practices work make them valuable in a sales environment. They also may be hired by corporations as product researchers and corporate educators, working with manufacturers to make their products better.

Public Health Dental Hygienists

Public health dental programs are funded by the government or nonprofit organizations to provide valuable services to those who would otherwise not obtain dental care. Head Start programs, local health departments, and rural or inner city com-

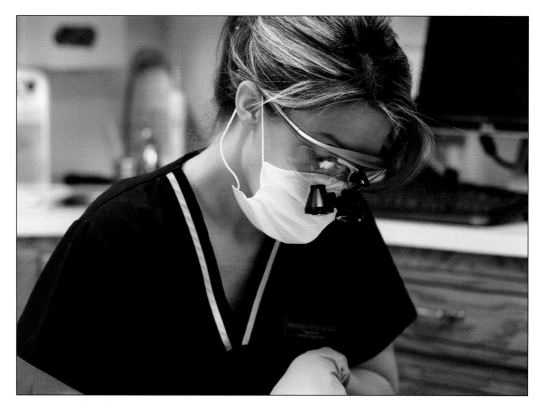

A dental hygienist wearing some of the specialized equipment that helps her do her job.

munity clinics all have a need for dental hygienists as clinicians, administrators, or researchers.

Researchers

Dental hygienists can conduct qualitative or quantitative research for colleges and universities, corporations, or government agencies to improve dental health programs. They can also influence the way other dental hygienists do their job by discovering new and better ways to maintain a patient's oral health or assist a general-practice dentist or a dental specialist.

Researchers are often asked to test a new procedure, product, or theory for accuracy or effectiveness.

Educators

Seasoned clinicians often choose to teach those studying to become dental hygienists about the processes and techniques used in the profession. Every college and university across the country that offers a dental hygiene program has instructors who staff that program. They must be familiar with educational theory so they can help students learn how to be competent dental hygienists. They must also stay up-to-date on the latest techniques in order to give students the best possible information.

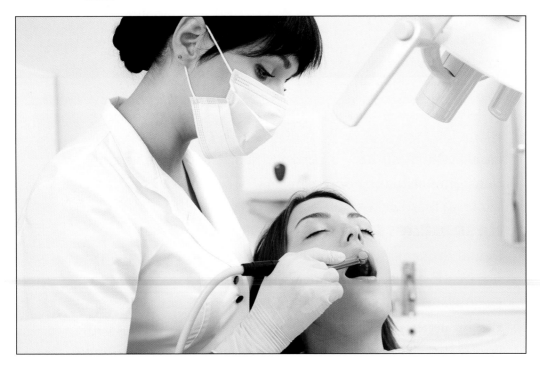

Polishing a patient's teeth.

Salary

The median annual wage for dental hygienists in May 2015 was just over $72,000. This means half of dental hygienists earned more than that amount and half earned less. Some dental hygienists also receive paid time off, sick leave, and retirement account contributions. However, these benefits are gen-

Educational Video

For a short video that shows how much a dental hygienist makes, scan here:

erally reserved for full-time employees. Nearly half of all dental hygienists work part time and are therefore ineligible for full-time benefits. The lowest-paid 10 percent of dental hygienists earned less than $50,000 and the highest-paid 10 percent earned more than $98,000 in 2015.

The top-paying states for dental hygienists in the United States are California, New Mexico, Nevada, and Washington, where the average salary is between $88,000 and $98,000. The states with the greatest demand for dental hygienists are Michigan, Oregon, Connecticut, Idaho, and Rhode Island, while California, Texas, New York, Florida, and Michigan employ the largest number of dental hygienists overall.

Career Advantages

Regardless of the settings in which they work, dental hygienists enjoy career advantages that are often unavailable in other professions. Not only do they gain personal satisfaction from giving people healthier smiles, there is prestige that goes along

Dental hygienists set patients at ease with their ability to explain procedures.

with being a dental hygienist. These professionals are highly sought-after members of the oral health care team, who are valued for their education and training. As a result, they may be asked to use their creativity while they are working with a wide variety of patients. Children have very different oral health care needs than adults, and the elderly and disabled each present challenges to a hygienist's ability.

Since they work when the dentist works, a dental hygienist's evenings and weekends are generally free. (Although many dentists have Saturday hours, often only the dentist is working during this time, not the dental hygienist.) Dental hygienists also enjoy a high level of job security. Recent studies have linked oral health to a person's overall health, giving people even more reason to take care of their teeth. Conditions such as heart disease, pregnancy, diabetes, osteoporosis, and HIV/AIDS are all affected by a person's oral health. As a result, more people are seeking dental care as part of their preventive health routines, generating a greater demand for professionals who can attend to these patients.

 Text-Dependent Questions

1. In what ways does an orthodontic dental hygienist differ from a general-practice dental hygienist?
2. What contributions do dental hygienists who are researchers make to the profession?
3. How are dental health and overall health connected?

 Research Project

Conduct online research to determine the average salary of dental hygienists in your area. Then, search available jobs for dental hygienists in your area. What education is required? How many years of experience? Are the jobs part time or full time? Are benefits like health insurance and retirement contributions offered?

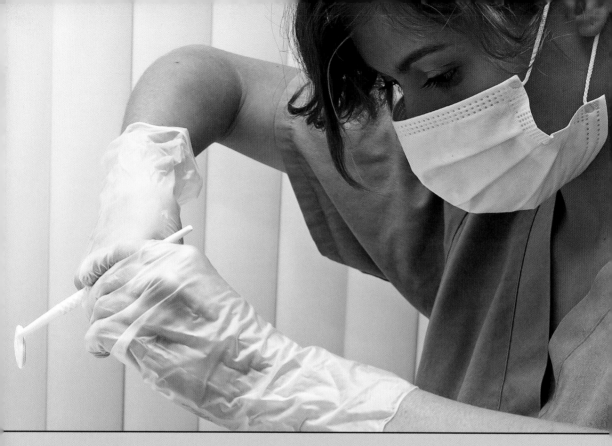

Dental hygiene students have an opportunity to practice their skills in a clinic under the supervision of an instructor.

 Words to Understand in This Chapter

accredited—referring to a school program that has been officially recognized as providing students with the level of education they will need to succeed.

licensure—the process of giving licenses to practice to professionals.

radiology—the branch of science dealing with x-rays.

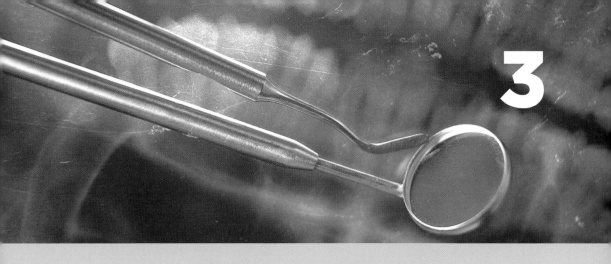

Education and Training

I t is impossible to do all of the things a dental hygienist does without the proper training and certification. In most cases, it takes a minimum of two years of education, ending in an associate's degree, to become a dental hygienist. These degrees can be obtained through a community college, an applied technology college, or a traditional university. Bachelor's and master's degrees in dental hygiene are often required to teach in the field, conduct research, or become a program administrator, but are less common among clinicians. These degrees are generally earned through colleges and universities with an emphasis in health sciences.

There are currently more than 300 *accredited* dental hygienist education programs in the United States. Each of these programs must comply with requirements set forth by the

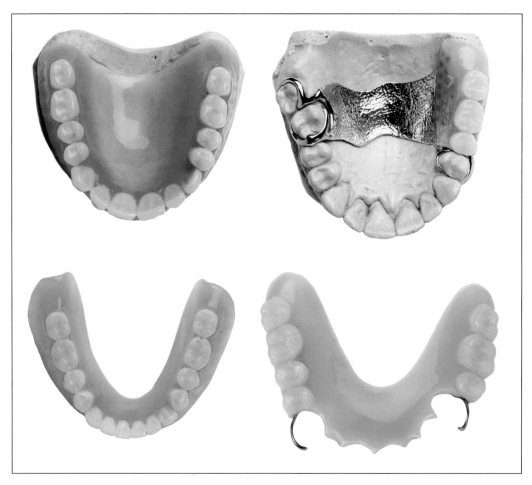

Hygienists who work in specialty dentist offices, such as periodontists, orthodontists, or endontists, receive specialized on-the-job training to assist dentists in complex procedures.

Commission on Dental Accreditation, the same organization that regulates educational programs for dentists. The requirements for accreditation are not easy to maintain and involve the number of instructors on staff, the types of classes taught, and the number of students who graduate and pass the certification exam. Students must graduate from an accredited dental hygienist education program in order to take the national certification exam.

Before being admitted into the dental hygiene program, students can expect to take college-level classes in chemistry, biology, math, psychology, and English. Then, they can apply for admission to the dental hygiene program, where they

Educational Video

Scan here for a short video on how to become a dental hygienist:

will take classes in *radiology*, ethics, and dental anatomy. As part of the training program, students are also expected to complete several clinical rotations, in which they will gain experience in an actual dental office or clinic. It is here that hygienists will have an opportunity to practice the skills they are learning in the classroom. Many dental hygiene programs offer free or low-cost dental services to other students on campus and people in the surrounding community in exchange for letting advanced students practice their skills. These clinical sessions are supervised by an instructor who can refine a dental hygienist's technique on an actual patient. Accredited dental hygiene programs require an average of nearly 3,000 clinical experience hours before awarding a degree in dental hygiene. This ensures that hygienists are confident in their skills before taking their certification exam and entering the workforce.

Licensure

Once you have completed your education in dental hygiene,

you are required to take the National Board Dental Hygiene Examination in order to become a licensed dental hygienist. *Licensure* protects the safety of the public by greatly reducing the likelihood that someone without training would attempt to do the job of a dental hygienist.

Every state has a different licensing requirement for dental hygienists. This means if a dental hygienist moves from one state to another, he has to reapply for licensing in his new state. However, most states' requirements follow a similar pattern. A person must:

1. Graduate from an accredited dental hygiene program.
2. Take and pass the written National Board Dental Hygiene Examination.
3. Complete a regional or state clinical board examination.

The National Board Dental Hygiene Examination is a 350-question written test, divided into two parts. The first part tests a person's knowledge of the science classes she has taken in her course of study. It also asks questions about her dental hygiene classes and how well she remembers the information she learned there. The second part is a series of questions based on several case studies. Here a person must be able to apply all of his knowledge to real-life situations. For both parts of the written exam, a person can consult his lecture notes and text-books for references.

The regional or state clinical board examination is a little different from the national written test. While the tests vary slightly, all of them test a person's ability to treat patients in a

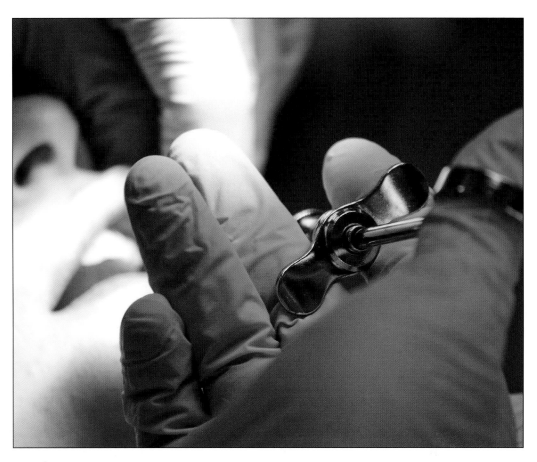

Giving anesthesia is a process that takes training and practice.

clinical setting. Some may have a written or computer-based portion, but overall these exams are designed to make sure a dental hygienist is not only educated, but skilled in the job as well.

Continuing Education

Becoming a licensed dental hygienist is not something that happens just once. Each state requires dental hygienists to

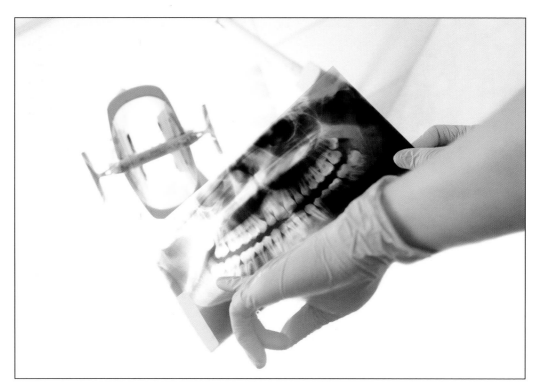

Learning how to take and read x-rays is an important element of a dental hygienist's education.

apply for licensure every one to three years. Most health care professions require licensed practitioners to complete additional classes throughout their career to keep abreast of changes to techniques, procedures, and licensing requirements. These requirements are called continuing education.

While continuing education requirements for renewing a dental hygienist's license vary from state to state, those working in the field have several options to complete them. They may take classes at a college or university toward a bachelor's or master's degree. In fact, many dental hygienists find that over the course of several years they are able to complete an advanced degree simply by meeting their continuing education requirements. Dental hygienists may attend conferences on new techniques and the latest research in the field as part of their continuing education. They may take online classes through a variety of accredited educational outlets that give them further insight into their job. Regardless of the method, dental hygienists must keep track of their continuing education hours so they can submit proof of having completed them to their state licensing board when the time comes for renewal of their license.

Many states allow dental hygienists to substitute a number of continuing education hours for service hours. Dental hygienists may spend 5 to 30 hours providing dental services to those who normally don't have access to care in one of several authorized locations. Since each state varies in its requirements for licensure, some states do not allow dental hygienists to trade service for continuing education.

What You Can Do to Be Ready

While the requirements for becoming a dental hygienist may seem daunting, it is a very manageable process when it is taken one step at a time. Academic advisers at colleges and universities are there to guide you through the process, helping you select the right classes in the best order. Tutoring is often available for help with difficult subjects. Instructors and professors offer office hours where they are available to answer questions.

The best preparation for a dental hygiene program is to take classes in high school that will give you a basic understanding

A Surgeon General's report released in 2000 drew the connection between a person's overall health and their oral health.

of what you will study. Classes in biology, chemistry, math, English, psychology, and physiology all work together to pre-pare students for the rigors of studying health care at a college level. While you may be required to take many of these same subjects in college, your studies in high school will give you a basic understanding of the material and help you to succeed.

Thoroughly check out the colleges or universities you are considering applying to. Ask questions about the types of class-es they require for admission into the dental hygiene program. Find out what their graduation rate is and how many of their graduates are currently working in the field. Ask about their first-time pass rate on the National Board Dental Hygiene Examination. This will tell you whether their program does a good job of preparing their students for the exam. Look at their tuition and fees, ask questions about financial aid, and consider whether you want to remain close to home or go away to school. All these factors will come into play as you decide which college, university, or applied technology college is right for you.

 Text-Dependent Questions

1. Why is it important to receive your dental hygiene education at an accredited college or university?
2. What are some ways that dental hygienists can complete their continuing education requirements?
3. What are some steps you can take now to be ready to enter a dental hygiene program?

 Research Project

Contact your local colleges, universities, or applied technology colleges to find out about their dental hygiene programs. Ask what you must do to be accepted. Find out if there are special prerequisites you need to have or classes you need to take prior to applying. Ask what their graduation rate is, how they can help you find a job after you finish your education, and what percentage of graduates are currently working in the field. Find out what the tuition rates are and what sort of financial aid is available.

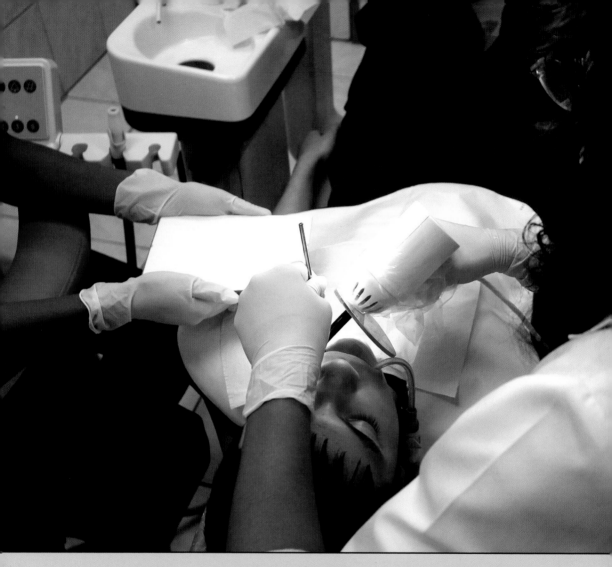

Technology plays an important role in dentistry today.

 Words to Understand in This Chapter

sealant—material used for sealing something so as to make it airtight or water-tight.

underserved populations—people who have limited options when it comes to health care, dental care, or education.

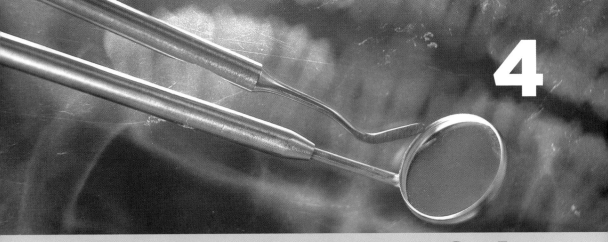

The Evolution of the Dental Hygienist Profession

As a student looking into becoming a dental hygienist, you are preparing to join more than 300,000 people in one of the fastest-growing realms of health care today. With recent studies linking a person's dental health to overall health, record numbers of people are seeking dental care. As a result, dentists are hiring dental hygienists in record numbers to assist them in their efforts to care for people's oral health, teeth, and gums. While their services are in high demand today, dental hygienists have been caring for people's oral health for most of the last century.

Early Dental Hygienists

The first record of dental hygienists cleaning people's teeth shows up in the late 1880s. Then known as "dental nurses,"

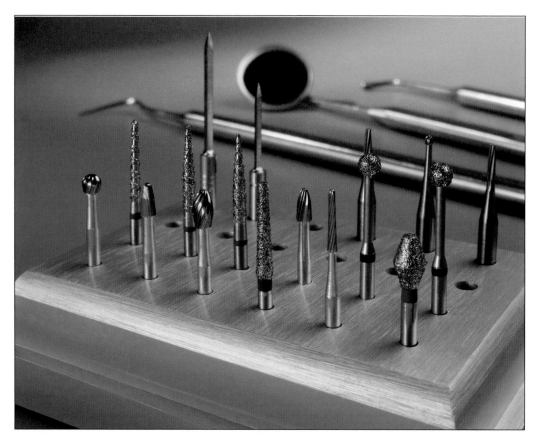

A dental hygienist has to be familiar not only with their tools, but with a dentist's tools as well.

their primary focus was to help dentists perform extractions. Since oral hygiene was different than it is today, regular dental cleaning was not part of the dental nurse's job. By 1906, a dentist by the name of Alfred C. Fones trained his assistant, Irene Newman, to act as an apprentice. At the time she would scale tartar off teeth and polish them. Since Dr. Fones disliked the term "dental nurse," he was the one who coined the job title "dental hygienist." Other dentists at the time were also training their assistants to clean teeth, but no formal educational program was offered in the United States.

In 1910, the Ohio College of Dental Surgery was the first college to offer formal "dental nurse" classes, amid some controversy. Dentists in Ohio did not like the idea that dental nurses would be trained to do something that was considered the job of the dentist. As a result, they opposed any formal training that would teach a dental hygienist how to clean teeth. Many of the dental nurses who completed their training at the Ohio College of Dental Surgery were never allowed to practice. The training program eventually closed.

Dr. Fones did not allow the closing of the Ohio College's dental nursing program to deter him in his pursuit of a profession he felt was worthwhile. Over the course of the next several years, he trained 97 dental hygienists who were licensed and allowed to practice. Connecticut was the first state to allow

Dental hygienists were once known as "dental nurses." While the term isn't used today, dental hygienists often fill the nursing role in dentistry.

licensure of dental hygienists, in 1915. However, many dentists in the area were afraid to give dental hygienists duties that could bleed over into the functions they performed themselves. The state scaled back the types of tasks hygienists could do. Many states followed Connecticut's lead and dental hygienists throughout the country came to be regulated by dentists.

In September 1923 the American Dental Hygienists Association (ADHA) was formed. This gave dental hygienists a way to advance the profession, develop new career paths, provide training, and support each other. It also created a platform for dental hygienists to gather as a group and have their voices heard as one body.

Dental Hygiene in the 1960s

A lot of important firsts for the profession occurred in the 1960s. The first version of the national board exam for dental hygienists was given in April 1962. The first male dental hygienist graduated from college in 1965. It was also during the 1960s that fluoride became a standard treatment for fighting tooth decay and the first electric toothbrush was sold in the United States.

For the profession as a whole, the 1960s brought about two key advances. First, in 1965 the American Dental Hygienists Association created bylaws to allow for men to become licensed, practicing dental hygienists. Up to this point, the profession had been dominated by women and men were not allowed to participate in the ADHA, the professional organization. This move toward equality opened up opportunities for more men to become dental hygienists.

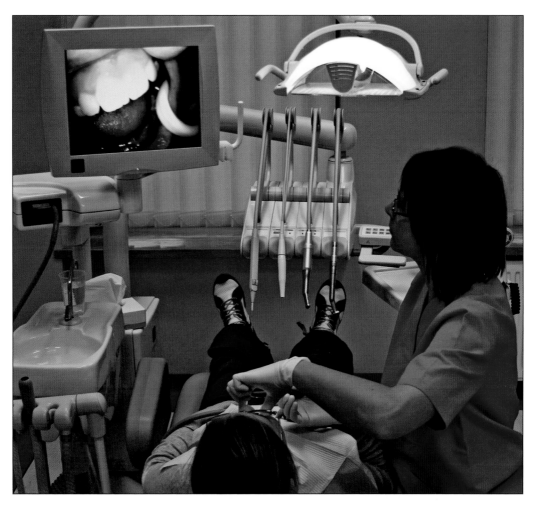

A dental hygienist uses an intra-oral camera to show the patient what they are seeing.

In 1967, the ADHA also formulated continuing-education recommendations. This move provided incentives for dental hygienists to continually learn new techniques, new technologies, and new ways of doing their jobs. Today, continuing education plays a vital role in the periodic relicensure of dental hygienists around the country.

Educational Video

For a lesson on dental hygiene, scan here:

Dental Hygiene in the 1970s

In the 1970s the National Board exam began to change from one that merely tested a person's knowledge to one that also tested the ability to use that knowledge. This change paved the way for the exam that is offered by the National Board today. Currently, it is divided into two parts—one that asks questions about the things students learned in a classroom, and one that requires students to use their knowledge in fictional case studies. While the National Board exam in the 1970s began to test students' ability to apply their knowledge in made-up scenarios, the current two-part exam was not created until 1998.

During this time, *sealants* were widely adopted to prevent cavities. Many hygienists began wearing pants to work instead of dresses. Ultrasonic scalers became popular for removing tartar without needing as much pressure. But the biggest change happened when, in the state of Washington, dental hygienists were first allowed to administer a local anesthetic. This practice, previously reserved for dentists, is now accepted practice in 44 states where trained dental hygienists can administer anesthetic to patients.

The Last 50 Years

While the 1960s and 1970s were a time for growth and development in the profession, the 1980s and 1990s saw the expansion of the dental hygienist's scope of practice. In 1984, the state of Washington became the first place where dental hygienists could practice unsupervised in specific settings. This allowed them to practice in hospitals, nursing homes, and other settings where people were unable to travel to a dentist's office for routine oral care. It also set the stage for later laws allowing dentists to hire multiple hygienists to perform diagnostic testing and dental cleanings in a collaborative environment. Today, many dental practices employ multiple dental hygienists to offer routine care while the dentist performs examinations and more involved procedures.

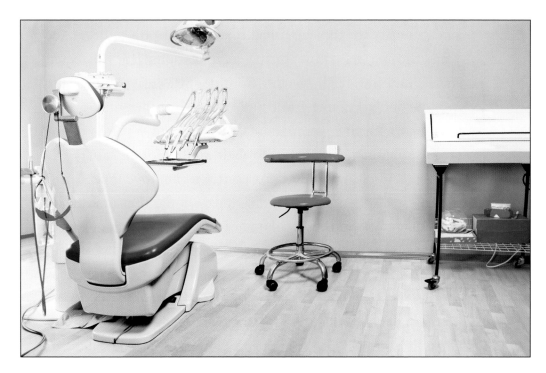

A modern dentist's office is equipped with a variety of tools to make a dental hygienist's job easier.

The early 21st century saw the dawn of the era of cosmetic dentistry. Advances in caps, veneers, crowns, bridges, and implants made healthy, straight, beautiful smiles accessible to all, regardless of genetics. As a result, many dental hygienists began receiving training on caring for cosmetic dental work as well as assisting in the placement of these devices.

One of the more significant advances in the last 30 years is the publication of "Oral Health in America: A Report from the Surgeon General." Published in 2000, this report, released by the U.S. Department of Health, was the first of its kind to link people's oral health to their overall health. Until that time, oral health was assumed to be important for the function of a person's mouth alone. With the surgeon general's report, a medical authority for the first time linked oral health to heart and lung disease, premature birth, complications from diabetes, stroke, and low birth weight. Routine, preventive oral health care suddenly became front and center in a person's overall health care routine, and patients who had not visited a dental professional in years flocked to their dentist for cleanings, fillings, screenings, and other procedures to improve their dental health. Since then, other studies have shown that oral health plays a key role in the likelihood of infection in other areas of the body, especially in the head and neck.

The Future of Dental Hygienists

The number of dentists graduating from accredited programs is beginning to decrease. For the first time in decades, dentists looking to retire do not have enough dentists to replace them. Over the next decade, states that require dental hygienists to practice in collaboration with dentists will face the problem of too many patients to care for and two few dentists to provide that care. In response, many states have adopted laws that allow dental hygienists to practice without the collaboration or supervision of a dentist. This trend is likely to continue as fewer dentists are entering the field for dental hygienists to collaborate with.

It is also likely that dental hygienists will see the emergence of better, newer technology as advances continue in the types of tools available to them. They are also likely to see an increase in nontraditional care settings that will allow them to care for *underserved populations* on site, rather than making the people come to them. In all, it is an exciting time to be a dental hygienist.

 Text-Dependent Questions

1. How did the dental hygiene profession take shape in the early 1900s?
2. Why did dentists first object to having dental hygienists clean teeth?
3. How did the surgeon general's report shape oral health care today?

 Research Project

Talk to a dental hygienist who has been practicing for more than ten years. Ask her how the profession has changed over that time. Ask what she sees as the future of the profession. Write a two-page paper based on your research and present it to the class.

A shortage of dentists in some parts of the country has opened up opportunities for dental hygienists to provide direct access care. In thirty-eight states dental hygienists can provide routine oral care, such as cleanings and x-rays, without the supervision of a dentist.

 Words to Understand in This Chapter

legislation—laws adopted by either states or the federal government.

psychology—the scientific study of the mind and behavior.

repetitive motion injuries—injuries to the body that may be caused by tasks that are repeated over and over again; they may also be caused by vibrations, mechanical compression, or maintaining awkward positions.

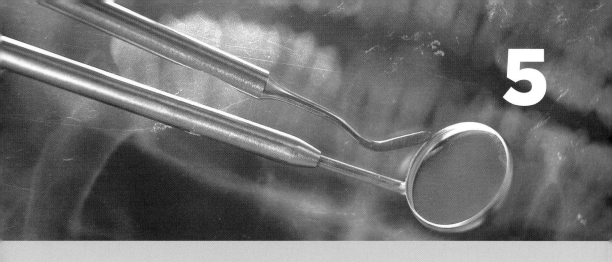

Overview
and Interview

The demand for dental hygienists is expected to increase over the next ten years by 19 percent. This is more than the average of any other professions in the United States. A dental hygienist makes an average of more than $72,000 a year with the highest-paid dental hygienists living in California, New Mexico, Nevada, and Washington. Nearly half of all dental hygienists work part time and in many cases work for more than one dentist.

While an associate's degree from an accredited dental hygiene program is required, and all dental hygienists must pass the National Dental Hygiene Board Examination, state requirements for the licensure of dental hygienists vary. Dental hygienists must be certified to practice in the state where they live. Bachelor's and master's degrees in dental hygiene are available at many colleges and universities, but those who have advanced degrees tend to focus less on clinical work and more on instruction or administration.

A dental hygienist shows her patient the correct way to brush his teeth.

Q&A with a Professional in the Field

Tawna Lewis

What follows is the transcript of an interview with Tawna Lewis, a dental hygienist working in the field. Currently pursuing a master's degree in dental hygiene and working part time for a dentist in a small city, Tawna discussed her 23-year career and how she thinks the profession will change over the next decade.

Question: How long have you been working as a dental hygienist?

Tawna: I graduated from college in 1993 and started working for a dentist in California, so I've been doing this for more than 23 years.

Question: What inspired you to get into this field?

Tawna: Growing up, my dad was a dentist. I started working for him, cleaning his office, when I was twelve or thirteen. Even all the way through high school I knew this was what

I wanted to do. It was just a matter of putting my dream into action.

Question: What kinds of classes did you take in college?

Tawna: I took a lot of sciences, of course—chemistry, biology, things like that. I also had to take English and *psychology*. I think a lot of people don't realize just how important good communication skills are in dental hygiene. Not only do you have to be able to explain procedures in a way patients can understand, but you have to understand what may be holding patients back from taking care of themselves. That's where the psychology comes into play. Once I was accepted into the dental hygiene program, I started studying specific procedures and techniques. We also had to complete several clinical classes where we had an instructor sitting with us while did the things we had been learning in class.

Question: Where did you work just after graduation?

Tawna: I was really lucky. My husband and I moved to California, where I'm from, and I started working for a dentist there. She had been a dental hygienist for many years and at age 40 had decided to go back to school to become a dentist. Working for her was the greatest experience I could have had right out of school. She pushed me in a way that other dentists haven't since. She understood exactly what my job was because she had done it for so many years. She really was and still is a great mentor to me.

Question: What has been the most challenging aspect of the job?

Tawna: I don't think a lot of people understand the physical toll it takes on your body. Positioning and *repetitive motion injuries* are very common in dental hygiene. You develop aches and pains in your shoulders and back from bending over your patients so much. You may develop carpal tunnel syndrome in your wrists from using the tools. Fortunately, dental hygiene programs are addressing ways to avoid these types of injuries. They are teaching students how to better position their bodies so they are more comfortable and how to avoid injury. I have developed some of those aches and pains over the years that make it difficult to work as a clinician full time. That definitely played a part in my decision to go back and get a master's degree.

Knowing how the food you eat affects your teeth is an important part of a dental hygienist's education.

Question: Speaking of your master's degree, what is your career goal once you complete it?

Tawna: I have been a clinical instructor for many years and I love it! My goal is to become an instructor at the local university so I can take all the things I have learned over my career and help mentor new dental hygienists.

Question: What has been the most rewarding aspect of the job?

Tawna: Helping people, without a doubt. As a dental hygienist you get to develop relationships with people over years. You watch the kids grow up and have children of their own. You see people change their habits in an effort to become healthier. Those relationships and helping a person live a healthier life is the best part of my job.

Question: Looking back over your career, what has changed the most over time?

Tawna: I think the biggest thing that has changed is how dental hygienists are viewed. When I was going through school, I had an instructor say that we were just "the cleaning ladies." That's it. We were there to clean teeth and nothing more. That attitude has changed a lot over time, especially with recent studies that have linked oral health to a person's overall health. It makes sense, though. The mouth is not a separate system. Of course the bacteria in the mouth will have an effect on the rest of the body. So now, we are not just the cleaning ladies, we're patient educators. We are

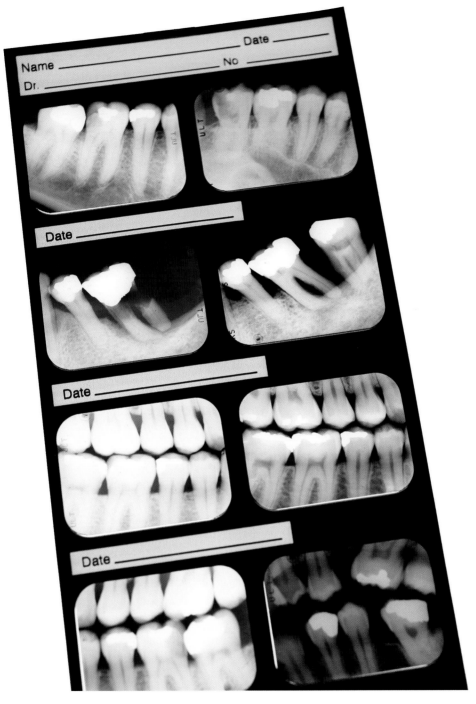

Digital x-rays are an exciting new technology in dental hygiene. Not only can a dentist or hygienist see the x-ray right away, he or she can quickly show the patient their own teeth.

helping people understand how taking care of their mouth is another step in taking care of their health.

Question: In my research, I found that at one time dental hygienists were called "dental nurses." While that's not necessarily the term used today, is it fair to compare you to nurses in your role in the dentist's office?

Tawna: Absolutely. Look at what nurses do—they run diagnostic tests, they explain diagnoses to patients, they teach them how to take better care of themselves. We do all the same things, but we are focused on the mouth, rather than on the rest of the body.

Question: What role has technology played in your career?

Tawna: There are two pieces of technology I have been very excited about. The first is digital x-ray. Years ago we took a two-by-three-inch (5-cm x 7.5-cm) film of someone's teeth and had to try to show them the problems we were seeing in a very small picture. Now, we can take a digital x-ray, blow it up 200 times its size, and show someone on a screen exactly where the problem is. The second is using digital cameras in the mouth to show patients, in color and in real time, what is going on inside their mouth. It takes something very abstract—decay, abscess, anything—and makes it personal to the patient. When you have a problem with your car and you take it to the mechanic, he will generally tell you what is wrong. And you have to go on faith that what he is telling you is right. For years, we have been doing the same thing with our patients. We might say that they have decay in a spot and need a filling, but they have to take our word for it. We don't have to do that anymore. It really is amazing how people pay attention to a problem when you can show them a picture of it.

Question: What kind of personal traits do you think are important for a dental hygienist?

Tawna: You have to like people. This is not a profession you can be good at if you don't like people. You have to have a lot of patience with them. Some will change their behavior because they understand that you are trying to help them be healthier, and some won't. You have to be able to treat the ones that won't change with the same compassion as the ones who do.

Maintaining a friendly demeanor is an important element of a dental hygienist's job.

Question: What advice would you give to someone who is considering a career as a dental hygienist?

Tawna: Don't give up. Some dental hygiene programs are extremely competitive and it may take applying two or even three times to get in. If this is what you want to do, don't give up on it just because you don't get in on the first try. It's a wonderful career. I can provide well for my family. The hours you work are great, especially if you have kids. You don't generally work nights or weekends. I have loved being a dental hygienist.

Question: Where do you see the career in ten years?

Tawna: I think the most exciting part of what is happening in the profession is the *legislation* allowing dental hygienists to work without a dentist in places like nursing homes and adult day-care centers. Nursing homes are a prime example of a population that doesn't have the access to dental care they need. Oftentimes, they cannot care for their own teeth. They are receiving physical therapy or occupational therapy or medical attention, but medical assistants are not as well-trained as dental hygienists to provide oral care. What the new legislation does is allow dental hygienists to practice in these types of settings without the supervision or collaboration of a dentist. The same could be said for school districts in poor areas where kids don't have access to a dentist. Dental hygienists could work alongside a nurse for a school or a district to provide patient education, basic cleaning services, or even simple things like toothbrushes and floss to kids who wouldn't otherwise have them.

It also would not surprise me if, in the next ten years, dental hygienists are providing the majority of preventive oral care in their own practices and then referring patients to dentists for things like fillings. We are already doing the majority of the preventive care in dentists' offices. With fewer dentists graduating from dental school, there will have to be a shift somewhere to take some of the burden off them.

 Text-Dependent Questions

1. What advice does Tawna give to someone considering a career as a dental hygienist?
2. What two characteristics are important for someone to have in order to be successful as a dental hygienist?
3. What role does technology play in dental hygiene?

 Research Project

Go to the Bureau of Labor Statistics website. Look up the salary and trends for dental hygienists in your state.

Series Glossary

accredited—a college or university program that has met all of the requirements put forth by the national organization for that job. The official stamp of approval for a degree.

Allied Health Professions—a group of professionals who use scientific principles to evaluate, diagnose and treat a variety of diseases. They also promote overall wellness and disease prevention in support of a variety of health care settings. (These may include physical therapists, dental hygienists, athletic trainers, audiologists, etc.)

American Medical Association (AMA)—the AMA is a professional group of physicians that publishes research about different areas of medicine. The AMA also advocates for its members to define medical concepts, professions, and recommendations.

anatomy—the study of the structure of living things; a person and/or animal's body.

associate's degree—a degree that is awarded to a student who has completed two years of study at a junior college, college, or university.

bachelor's degree—a degree that is awarded to a student by a college or university, usually after four years of study.

biology—the life processes especially of an organism or group.

chemistry—a science that deals with the composition, structure, and properties of substances and with the transformations that they undergo.

cardiology—the study of the heart and its action and diseases.

cardiopulmonary resuscitation (CPR)—a procedure designed to restore normal breathing after cardiac arrest that includes the clearance of air passages to the lungs, mouth-to-mouth method of artificial respiration, and heart massage by the exertion of pressure on the chest.

Centers for Disease Control—the Centers for Disease Control and Prevention (CDC) is a federal agency that conducts and supports health promotion, prevention and preparedness activities in the United States with the goal of improving overall public health.

diagnosis—to determine what is wrong with a patient. This process is especially important because it will determine the type of treatment the patient receives.

diagnostic testing—any tests performed to help determine a medical diagnosis.

EKG machine—an electrocardiogram (EKG or ECG) is a test that checks for problems with the electrical activity of your heart. An EKG shows the heart's electrical activity as line tracings on paper. The spikes and dips in the tracings are called waves. The heart is a muscular pump made up of four chambers.

first responder—the initial personnel who rush to the scene of an accident or an emergency.

Health Insurance Portability and Accountability Act (HIPAA)—a federal law enacted in 1996 that protects continuity of health coverage when a person changes or loses a job, that limits health-plan exclusions for preexisting medical conditions, that requires that patient medical information be kept private and secure, that standardizes electronic transactions involving health information, and that permits tax deduction of health insurance premiums by the self-employed.

internship—the position of a student or trainee who works in an organization, sometimes without pay, in order to gain work experience or satisfy requirements for a qualification.

kinesiology—the study of the principles of mechanics and anatomy in relation to human movement.

Master of Science degree—a Master of Science is a master's degree in the field of science awarded by universities in many countries, or a person holding such a degree.

obesity—a condition characterized by the excessive accumulation and storage of fat in the body.

pediatrics—the branch of medicine dealing with children.

physiology—a branch of biology that deals with the functions and activities of life or of living matter (as organs, tissues, or cells) and of the physical and chemical phenomena involved.

Surgeon General—the operational head of the US Public Health Department and the leading spokesperson for matters of public health.

Further Reading

Aulie, Nancy. *Career Diary of a Dental Hygienist*. Marietta, GA: Garth Gardner Company, 2007.

Finn, Heather. *Fabulous Farrah and the Sugar Bugs*. New York: Little Harbor Books, 2016.

Young, Ben. *The Joy of Flossing*. North Charleston, S.C.: CreateSpace Independent Publishing, 2014.

Internet Resources

www.dentistryiq.com
The web's most comprehensive resource for dentistry professionals.

www.mouthhealthy.org
Informative website by the American Dental Association.

www.ada.org
The American Dental Association website has information on the outlook for dental hygienists.

www.rdhmag.com
This is the website of a professional magazine for registered dental hygienists.

Publisher's Note: The websites listed on this page were active at the time of publication. The publisher is not responsible for websites that have changed their address or discontinued operation since the date of publication. The publisher reviews and updates the websites each time the book is reprinted.

Index

Numbers in ***bold italic*** refer to captions.

About the Author

Jennifer Hunsaker grew up wanting to become a pediatric surgeon specializing in cleft palate repair. Instead, she earned a Bachelor's Degree in Communicative Disorders and a Master's Degree in Human Resource Management and went on to work as a consultant for small businesses. Unsatisfied by the business world, she returned to her first love as a writer of medically-related content geared toward children, students, and those who work with them. When she isn't writing, she is chasing her husband, four children, and Yorkie named Wookie through the mountains of Northern Utah.